DISCARDED
THIS IS NO LONGER PROPERTY OF THE SEATTLE PUBLIC LIBRARY

CHURCH OF THE EXQUISITE PANIC

THE OPHELIA POEMS

Carole Glasser Langille

COPYRIGHT © 2012 Carole Langille

ALL RIGHTS RESERVED. No part of this book may be reproduced or transmitted in any form or by any means whatsoever without written permission from the publisher, except by a reviewer, who may quote brief passages in a review. For information, write Pedlar Press at PO Box 26, Station P, Toronto Ontario M5S 2S6 Canada.

ACKNOWLEDGEMENTS
The publisher wishes to thank the Canada Council for the Arts and the Ontario Arts Council for their generous support of our publishing program.

LIBRARY AND ARCHIVES CANADA
CATALOGUING IN PUBLICATION

Langille, Carole Glasser
    Church of the exquisite panic : the Ophelia poems / Carole Glasser Langille.

ISBN 978-1-897141-52-6

1. Ophelia (Fictitious character)--Poetry. I. Title.

PS8573.A557C58 2012   C811'.54   C2012-905707-X

COVER ART Maryanna Hardy, *Drowning Girl*, 2008
BOOK DESIGN Zab Design & Typography, Toronto

TYPEFACES
Galliard Carter & Cone (body)
Gotham (titles)

Printed in Canada

*Again, to Bill
and to Caleb and Luke*

9   Plough

I

13 Ophelia's Barter
14 Murder
15 The Bog
17 Spy
18 A Letter
19 Though He's Dead
20 Red
21 Cock
22 Horses
23 Who Is the Lender, Who the Borrower?
24 Hole
25 The Dress I Wore
27 Stir

II

31 Yahrzeit
33 Zero
34 The Movie
35 Andy Warhol Paints Ophelia
36 Ophelia's Interview with Carl Jung
37 When He Crossed the Field

III

41 Church of the Exquisite Panic,
42 *Thou Art With Me*
43 The Ocean Did Not
44 The Prison of Decorum Will Not Admit You
45 Heart's Oven
47 Not

48	Mother
49	The Four Agreements
50	Crows
51	Directions
52	Monarchs
53	Consecration
54	I Wanted to Learn to Touch You
55	What They Thought
56	Should Two Arms Lift Me
57	Fine
58	The Old Man
59	You Win
60	Bearing
61	ophelia.com

65	Girls Who Lived in New York in the Sixties
69	Little Sister
70	Syndrome
73	Kimberly Rogers
74	Black
75	To Break Away
79	Sex (or When We Were Young)

83	Memo
84	For a Drowned Woman
85	What I Could Have Learned by the Light of Misfortune
86	Nothing Held You

PLOUGH

When plough blades turn soil,
loamy earth falls into furrows.
The solitary bittern skulks by the shore. Motionless,
a heron waits for prey. Why should regret linger?
The silent frost-covered fields,
white as a page, must be harrowed.
Because night can elide the haunted hours
but only so long. There are times when accuracy
is the opposite of candor.
But only so long. Don't pretend
you don't understand me. Stories, like secrets,
are never safe until they're told. When you're broken
open, even air can be healing. Hold fast.
You are not yet the person
you will be. Though under the vines, you are the flickering
and love's broad curved blade cuts through you.

OPHELIA'S BARTER

There was no one down any of the roads
who might have guided me. Just memory:
what I could not assume, what he could not assure,
all the loss that crammed my drafty heart,
oh cutthroat, last shred. I traded
the North Star for a sinking bough. To have charity always
in our mouths, isn't that the virtue?
The cut throat of dusk leaked milky light
then darkened until the whole winter sky with its
hunters and beasts, its lit dippers, somersaulted
below the water's surface, rippling.
A dead man's hand, the ice pick of water,
pried open my mouth. But I had already tasted
all I would taste.

        From where I lie now
I can see, as if through a window,
what divides affection from despair, hope
from love, bruised fruit that so often
falls. And forgiveness, its lost brother.

MURDER

Some believe only what they aren't told,
those lies ingrown in hate and blame.
Just try to stop a story that must unfold. Unfold
it will. But look what you can do with what's already named.
Have you watched men hold swords as if they held
no sword, known blades that have a life of their own? Not bold,
we're pigeons, loathe to leave our nests though surrounded by flame.

I feel my way, song by song, down the long
corridor looking for signs: the chosen
from the choosing, right from strong.
One cannot force a word to rhyme, much as we'd like,
or pretend wrong isn't wrong
or insist God create the world many times. Do you still believe
you control what you control, my Lord?

THE BOG

Strange you should ask me to meet you
where branches cover stagnant water. Though perhaps
not *that* strange. Wondrous things flourish
in a place like this: ghost orchids, lilies that glow
phosphorescent at dusk.
Sun leaks through cold. Silence is intimate
as a kiss desired, not yet given. It is here
you placed your lips on my palm,
surprised me by taking, for a moment, one of my fingers
in your mouth.

Most private of all –
this opening we find ourselves in
and the far-off bird cry we hear, which sounds
as if it comes
from inside ourselves. When your hand
grazed my throat
my pulse thrummed. On such a night
you shared your secret. I believe of course
that the vision you saw,
wandering the world's edge, was real
as I am.

As you are beloved,
will-o'-the-wisp, friar's lantern,
who guides me to water
both bitter and sour. When I squint
I see you from the corner

of my stare and lower and raise you
out of this bog, so briny and filled
with tannin, it preserves everything
that falls inside.

SPY

A sentinel watches but a spy
remembers. The difference between
looking and seeing is the moment you close
your eyes. The spy recalls every exit and entrance, each
screened trap, all nervous smiles. Secretly, he knows
where the corpse of love lies buried and which self
is guilty before the murder's done. Even as he shows
his tact, he designs himself
to be overlooked, plans
what to tell and not say. Watching, he makes sure
not too much enters and nothing's removed
from the well of himself. A spy's his own warden
pacing the floor. Is there light flashing
from the dark? The spy's the self that quenches the spark.

A LETTER

Today I walked until I came upon a lit building and, entering,
saw it was a church
where a woman with a child prayed. It was tall
as a two-storey house. That everyone has two stories,
I am certain: *what is* and *what is imagined,* and though we long
to lay a pattern, like a chorale upon our lives,
there are more incongruities than rhyme, more weight
than words can possibly bear. Each street
leads to the next, we judge one night against another
and so lose the particular violet blue,
the lemony balm, a violent wind's harmonic charm. My lord,
the path is worn. What I believe we find, if we endure,
are the many names of God. We know so few.

In the church with its worn floor I suddenly knew
that every house, like a woman, has bones,
blood, skin. What compassion
we must accord.

When next we find ourselves
together, I shall read to you the prayer that showed me
what colour is, how each speaks in one of God's
many voices. So bright, so near,
they dazzle. I no longer need
to strain my ears to hear.

May this honoured day delight you.

THOUGH HE'S DEAD

It's still possible to believe
I can walk into his room and sit
and never long to turn and see his face.

Take up where I left off, place
myself apart and nod and say what's fit
and never question if I've been deceived.

But sun withdraws its comfort bit by bit.
The night, once chilled, will calm and fill with grace.
Death's free. It nods and lets us leave

without excuse.

RED

Sky at dawn, a hemorrhage
seeping through wadded clouds.
Red: the bleeding away of what is most

precious. A master telling me: *give up*.
Loss is seeing the centre
of what is burning go cold. I lose

hours. Lose my ring in a lake.
Lose heart. Who knew the waters
were this deep? How the body

sacrifices then gives
in. Lightning striking each nerve,
hot, dry, a concentrated fire

pressing down. Clotting, pulsing:
that's what saturation is. And embarrassed
silence. Love is best when it catches you

by surprise: the bloodstone you placed
in my hand, its splotches like sun
sinking in the sea.

COCK

You strutted like a cock while I was doomed
to walk at dusk among trees,
my thoughts burning, and still
I could not find
my way. As if night were unconscious,
I went through its pockets: dry white sand
and cockle shells, luminous, reflecting moons.
Oh but they were funny,
the snatches of song I heard. *For some must watch
and some must wait.* I walked
till the first cock crowed, cockeyed,
dreaming I would find you in your boat,
unmoored, remembering
how you fell to such a study of my face. My brother was wrong,
your words gave more heat than light.
Let me say it again: Cock of the walk,
cock of the rock, cocksure,
the morning is cockshy, struggling to rid itself
of dream. By what shift did you decide to hold,
not me, but that which
would forever be withheld?
You brushed against me
even as you turned. Man who ate air,
here I am with your words
in my mouth, tongue-tied.
I would not have thought love could survive
so much scorn and sorrow.

HORSES

Here, days are all dressage
and formality. Horses asleep
on their feet in the field.
But we both know

horses are always wandering off.
I lose afternoons searching for them.
Nights exhaust me; I sweat
as if capturing stallions. Whose voice
whispers beyond the stable?

Wild hope tramples the land to mud
and I lose sight of you. Then I, myself,
become invisible. And still my heart,
and yours, has to keep beating. Send word.
Even rumour

is something I can cling to. *Run*,
you shouted once, as untamed horses
galloped toward me. But I held
my ground. To step out of their way
and move to safety, I thought I had

all the time in the world.

WHO IS THE LENDER, WHO THE BORROWER?

I wanted to follow him until I arrived
inside his life, though my presence
left him more and more

unmanned. Hope stranded me,
neither widow nor wife. But desire to run
taught me to wait. Now I go out at dusk

when there is no wind and walk
to the end of the point, but don't stay long.
It's good to admit, I have no ground on which to stand.

HOLE

Grass cloaks the hole
to the cellar. When light slants, I see
moss covering vulnerable
places. I know, firsthand,

how dreams get washed away
like soil when nothing is left
to hold them in place.
In the afternoon river, light diamonds

and shimmers. Vines trail from cypresses
and swing in the breeze. By what
is light parted? How deep in the hills
does the limestone reach? Let me tell you

this: even sun-filled water
remembers winter in the hot season, when desire
burns too quick and shines too bright.
Mine evaporates like salt water

from skin. The man I love? His mouth
was summer. That's all I'll say.
And this: the dark inside me
is what I fall into when my path ends

and I'm still here.

THE DRESS I WORE

He gave me bolts of muslin
from which I made dresses that swished

as I walked, like water on rocks
where young birds land.

When dresses grew thin, I cut cloth
into lengths and sewed coverings for pillows

stuffed with white down. I tore
strips into shreds when cases frayed

and from those rags made paper.
On one page I wrote, *Under my dress*

I shiver and await you and folded the scrap
beneath pillows. Dreams grew thin –

libraries with no books, rookery
no rooks. Goldbricks and buncos

at tables in gardens. What a wonderful flower
the hummingbird is. When it lands it blossoms

with berries. When it molts it is always
in danger. Who's safe? And still the world,

with him in it,
opened my arms.

Dreams move the sea. Even there,
I reached out as if I could grasp that man,

again and again,
wall of water that he was.

STIR

I can hide like a thief
but the heart is a cop at the crossroads
who forces me out in the open. Outside,
where the earth is seeded, day
cedes its place. Water has picked up
the last shred of light and carried it away. *Hush*.
Evening is a great brooding dog. I want to leave
and not be followed. If I know a psalm, it's this: journey
is a type of singing, suffused with dance,
sufficing. The Sufis had it right. No one
is refused. The great lie is this: that voyage means
going. Each time I venture out,
I am always led inward, stumbling, hurtling,
as if falling were succeeding. Who holds up
whom? No one steals away.

YAHRZEIT

Was Ophelia Jewish? She read what she saw
backward from right to left, like Hebrew,
knowing what came second
was often followed by what came first: men were ghosts
before they died.

Among qualities that possess
inerasable names – Wisdom, *Yah*;
power, *Gevurah*;
understanding, *Binah* –
she looked for traces of her family tree.

Aren't kindness and love meant to unite
like father and mother, even for orphans?
But who will be married?
Who will be tried? In that palace no minyan,
no love, no protection, no hope: there she was.

A code of our honour is written
in the book of life. Then it's burned.
In such a book is recorded
what her father gave and what he hid. By any name,
her yahrzeit was for her father.

In her own book she wrote on invisible paper
what even she couldn't read. Revisions were difficult.
What she sought

was private: like a bride going to mikvah
before her wedding, God and Ophelia alone in the river.
From such water
did she believe she would emerge pure?

ZERO

The beggar says nothing's accomplished when zero's involved, but aren't we all
debtors when confronted with that naught, that nada, a cypher
that makes the whole
house shake. The absence of something seduces
and betrays, holds
us hostage. How many ways we die
from it. People are hauled aboard or swept
away, lavish or hoard because of that quantity of no
importance, that presence of *nothing*
that penetrates the spirit and ties the hands, tightens
its grip, forces us to live
year after year at the lowest
possible temperature. Though where would we be without
that cavity, that tunnel burrowing deep
into the most shadowy
place? Her very name begins with it – a
nothingness that, no matter what it's added to,
it leaves forever unchanged. O of *only*,
of *open*. But slide the door a crack
and see the bottomless depth
of dark upon dark. How vulnerable we are
to that void between negative and positive through which,
once we free fall,
there is no landing.

THE MOVIE

Like all good stories
each life has a theme
which keeps playing over and over.
Summarized, the narrative might read:
*Couple attempt romance despite
family angst*. In the background, appalling
music. If you've seen the previews
you know what you're in for: mental illness
and family cover-up. Piercings, tattoos.
The ferment of Jihad. An odd case
where the movie would play better
if the plot were not so
familiar. Ophelia begins to see
and not see. It is the exact sort of turmoil
at which the director excels.
But here is where the movie,
or should we say, the life, offers least.
Beneath its epic sprawl, does anyone
know Ophelia? Does anyone know
anyone at all?

ANDY WARHOL PAINTS OPHELIA

or rather eight Ophelias printed on the same page
each with a different shade of lipstick from beige
to blood-orange red. He invited her to parties, hung
her painting next to photos of stars, was stung
when she didn't accept invitations. She preferred
watching skateboarders in the park as the light blurred.
He said, *You get exactly what you no longer crave.*
He said, *Being born is like being sold as a slave.*
His favourite phrase: *So what?* Such sore, bruised
words. Ones she would never use.
He liked talkers. Son of a miner, he preferred drip I.V.
to *feeling*, suspected he wasn't living but watching rerun TV.
She rarely talked. *In the play I am in, I hardly say a thing*
she thought. *A nothing, a no one, in love with a king.*

OPHELIA'S INTERVIEW WITH CARL JUNG

Royalty
A borrowed cloak, muddied, laid over soaking ground.

Song
The harbour in which my boat was moored.

Silence
What quenched my thirst.

Father
A leaky ship.

Brother
My pocket of air as the ship went down.

Betrayal
The child I tried to drown. *Grief:* My teacher.
Madness: The mother I found for myself.

Love
Nothing is borrowed.

Death
Everything I thought I'd borrowed was mine.

WHEN HE CROSSED THE FIELD

He wants what she has.
When he crossed a field of long yellow grass
recently free of snow,
he felt as if he were walking
over the thick matted coat of some straw-coloured beast
about to wake, its spine cracking
beneath him. The sky, the sun – what force do these have
compared to her? The most difficult song
is the one he wants to sing
though he does not yet know it.

He knows she is ice melting
in the cove, its silvery surface
a glossy shimmer of foil. When he edges himself
onto the ice, he walks further
from shore than he intended
to go. How far from real life
he knows himself to be.
But every river has its origin.
Every night upsets each day,
toppling trees in its wake.
What misgivings, what steep slopes
remain when the darkness recedes?
He imagines if she lingers she'll be drenched
in shade. *If we are tired isn't it because*
we have already walked a long way?
With its endless fields of pearled snow, carved

in blue, with its fierce wind and all that's lost
in wind – isn't longing
the most open border in the world?

CHURCH OF THE EXQUISITE PANIC,

my church. All the birds, chattering,
drained into my hymnal, snapped shut
and tossed away. *The power of the past:* our sermon.
How the dead destroy: our hymn.

So the succession of sleepless nights depends
on how wide and widely spaced
the gaps in our logic, two lovers who never kissed
dissecting each syllable of what was said

and unsaid. A passionate, impulsive man –
wild hair blowing, linen shirt open
smelling of talc. When he spoke,
half in his tongue

half in mine, half his grief
entered my mouth. What did I care
his words were cold? I saw
what lay beneath.

His lips so bitter, even I
began to talk in tongues.
Fugitive happiness.

THOU ART WITH ME

Thou art with me, the psalm reads and I admire such faith
as I look out over the field of sea to the endless horizon,
knowing the waters are a stage where a play
is performed. Clouds part like curtains, sun shines its spotlight
and, sure enough, a boat approaches upon which, let us say,
my fate resides.
Doesn't all destiny disrupt the most careful plans
and the lack thereof?
Perhaps it will be my luck that I will not be there
when my ship arrives. Good fortune
that the cargo be unloaded and the vessel embark
without me. There is a blackness
darker than evening, a darkness blacker
than the absence of light, a weight heavier
than any anchor.
And if the passengers and crew survive the storm
or perish, if no one understands
their lines, who can deny that both hope and hopelessness
fight their way through us, each embodying more force
than any wind in any sail. *Thou art with me,* I repeat
as if repetition itself were an act of faith addressing,
as I do, the source of all words,
all introductions and all final acts.

THE OCEAN DID NOT

hurl my ship
skyward, smack it hard

on a surge of breakers. The hull
that split, the keel that cracked, were not

mine. I never sailed an ocean.
I never sailed.

But as Laertes said, "Even as you tremble,
violent nature elicits

your strength." So it did. The play
had it wrong: no adventure, no daring,

no courage, no risk. I had all,
confined as I was to the walls of the court.

THE PRISON OF DECORUM WILL NOT ADMIT YOU

I'd like to remove my disguise
but it's like clothing I won't strip away,
though my garments grow more and more

transparent. In the glare of your blinding
humiliating misconception,
you disrobed me. What could I hide behind

but astonishment? Understand,
nothing is forgotten.
Not even the words

you did not speak.

HEART'S OVEN

Anger, that haunted untrustworthy servant
(he lies with his sister, I'm certain), coal
on his hands, gave us more than we wanted,
cajoling us. And right before my eyes, he stole you from me.
                                        Remarkable.
In that instant I learned
            what interested you.

The fire that scratches summer's bones
                        is over. Alone, I let my arguments
scatter in the river where
wishes are ashes.

Your voice,
which I hear when I turn my lantern,
is not as remote as I remember. It makes a pattern of dark and light
                        over the cover of poppies,
those bright orange bursts
            I bake in my heart's oven.

Such warm bread I sought to serve you.
        Picture me still flushed after baking.

You remember the words in scripture
about the eye offending. How does one cleanse,
            not the two nearsighted, but the third,
                                    invisible?

What I saw
before you saw it yourself,
               was your killing, killing
what you wanted to avenge.

That's why I longed to track you, hack my way
      through drifts and tunnels,
pluck you
            from all that was
vanishing, suture

the ragged hole. My tonic, my embrasure, astonishing
as I knew you were.

The man who drifts into the past,
            the woman who wanders into the future,
how do they find their way back?

NOT

This is not a competition,
it's a voyage. The water's
headstrong. Not a confrontation,
a quotation. A list of sources.
A waiting room, not a finish line.
Not trophies: bits of scrap.
This is not happiness,
it's hunger.
Do you like the sauce?
Shall I take it back?

MOTHER

A week before my twelfth birthday Mother sent me to a nunnery. When you're a child everyone handles you, turning your shoulders in the direction they think you should go. I spent my days at prayer and drawing a laurel that grew by my window. I thought of that laurel as Daphne, recently escaped from Apollo. Mother had explained how gods turned girls into trees.

I was in the garden drawing and paused to look up, when the sky clogged. What little light there was, filtered by haze, dimmed as sun slid behind bruised clouds.

Two days later my brother came to fetch me. He'd brought the new carriage. *Mother's dead,* he told me. I felt such chill then as I have never known and all at once I was certain of one thing. Not that I would have a bleak future, not that my future would be treacherous or lonely, but that I would have no future at all.

That death was the hinge of my life. Never would I get the chance to say goodbye. Absence hovered leaving its mark, like a smudge from burnt wood. Even now, my mother is more alive to me than days I endure. Which is why I still don't quite believe in death *or* in life. Or that there is much difference between a noisy tree and a silent girl.

THE FOUR AGREEMENTS

Anger will force you
into the streets, drag you
through torrential hours.

Revenge, that hidden scavenger
eluding capture
will exhaust you.

Indecision, like icy water
dams you. Even when *feeling*,
the blood of life, returns.

But unhappiness, that innocuous plant,
adheres to all three. Once rooted in the heart,
it kills.

CROWS

When they alight they're as dark as their shadows.
Thousands of birds.
What shall we do with this murder of crows?

Should we string them broken-necked from trees? Mow
off their heads? Something's unmasked in the breeze.
When they alight they're as dark as their shadows.

Gardens bleed light in the sun's orange glow.
Apples line bins. Pines sharpen air.
What shall we do with this murder of crows?

Both sides are his dark side. The blackest crow
throws his lot in with the rest: good luck, bad luck.
When they alight they're as dark as their shadows.

These omens mock us. There's nowhere to go
in Elsinore. If one crow's sorrow, what are a thousand?
What shall we do with this murder of crows?
When they alight they're as dark as their shadows.

DIRECTIONS

A crazy map
of bird prints – arrows
in the snow: seagulls pointing
where to go. And look –
under trees, blue shadows floating.

MONARCHS

The length of their journey
exceeds the months of their lives. No hours
of mourning. No *our* percussed
in the susurration
as they rise up in millions,
black and orange stained-glass
flutterings. Generations die off
before young return to skim the same
sun-gold pool.

So breaks in each life
are mirrored. As light
shuts. As day drains
of air. As breath goes out
of evening. The mirrored lake
over which they fly breaking
into fragments
of gold. Of gold. What fortune
time is. Shattering.

CONSECRATION

Nothing can conceal
the exaltation of trees. A pivot
between earth and heaven,
they're dervishes halted in prayer.
The harsher world diminishes

as each tree breathes.
Dralas against disbelief,
they're the Eucharist consumed
by the cool wind in the airy grate
through the open mouths
of houses.

I WANTED TO LEARN TO TOUCH YOU

You were lute music I played
until a string broke.

Midnight rooms I explored
until the candle faltered.

A blanket I wrapped myself in
though I woke chilled.

Had your door been open
I would have entered.

Now you pass through trees
and come out the air I breathe.

WHAT THEY THOUGHT

My lover predicted
I'd become his mother. My father demanded
an obedient daughter. My brother begged
that fear be my advisor. My mother, gone,
left a hollow vessel, fractured,
wanting to be filled. Only I knew
what was left of me and what I let slide,
unprotected, though my prayers. I wondered,
Why not Ophelia, deeply beloved?
It was the ferryman at the River Death
who said, *Now there'll be no more Ophelias
slipping from Ophelia.*

SHOULD TWO ARMS LIFT ME

It takes great skill
to be still. Like stained glass,
nettles and loosestrife crush and colour
the light streaming in.

In this Eden, should two arms lift me,
it looks as if I could still wake.
Wasn't I lovely? Here the wind
xylophones my skin. Light

chimes. Like a garment, I am turned
inside out, life balancing
on my floating bones. A pity
I have come to this place

of no pity. I let go of what I wanted
with such little force,
the very water
remained unbroken.

FINE

I wish I'd been told
how simple death is. For sleep,
it helps to have the moon
or a slip of it. For death, a moment
that tips and drains
and leaves us cold.

How warm this cold.
It's fine. I listen
as rain beats on the earth
above my head. So air and water mingle
in the grave. To give us
what we will not grasp
but can't refuse.

THE OLD MAN

When I die the old man who lives inside me
will give me his blessing
and tend my body.

I forced him to lie shivering
in cold water
and he forgave me.

Eyes lively, he will oil my feet,
smooth my hands.
Each moment I approach death

he grows younger, stronger.
"There's so much I wanted,"
I tell him. *Soon,* he says

you will want nothing. When I die
the old man who lives inside me
will be ready and willing with answers.

Though I, deep in his body
will need no answers.
I'll have no questions.

YOU WIN

burst of jittery light
blinking on off an ocean
announcing itself within
you shimmering witness you
win I tell myself
deciphering ciphers inside
outside Virgin Queen
of heaven strength at rest in her light the joy
of such a place to reside in outside
you within you you win you
holder of slim threads deeds you
pushed hard against the closed door
with all you had ordinary
dreams to amuse you
amused you greet your muse bowing
amazed you see the maze traversed
air in light versed in slight breezes you
scared sacred truly
you win unruly
you rallied rattled you
reasoned reprieved you witnessed
you win you win

BEARING

The Lord Our Saviour must have known
when he breathed the damp air
that sodden night in March and rain
eased the lane to its slippery
conversion, even He must have known
that my hope, if you call it that,
would be costly. Light slipped
out of the ordinary world leaving
the dark thick, oily. The earth slid
from soil to mud. Stones
made the road *razor*,
not road. Where did I hope
to arrive? In a world where love
was infinitesimal –
you'd miss it if you held your breath –
and faith was drafty, enormous,
did life offer anything (if not for Him,
then why for me?)
but death as the perfect fit?

OPHELIA.COM

Isn't a font
for holy water?
How many sites
float in my name? Jewellery, a rock band,
Shakespeare, of course, and Adolescent Girls. Virtue
drained into the virtual. I'm remembered
for the one act that will never
end, my interminable crossing over
into dark water.
Dying as I am continually,
everyone has use for me. The drive's hard.
Once barely perceptible,
now I'm perpetual.

GIRLS WHO LIVED IN NEW YORK IN THE SIXTIES

"Boys actually do that?" I asked
and looked up *cunnilingus*
in the dictionary, to make sure Marie was right. Then
I kept looking up the word.

I thought I knew a lot, I had
two older sisters. But Marie knew more.
She knew silence
would keep our secrets for us,

but words allowed wildness.
They made the act come alive
without having to submit
to the world.

I knew a lot of poets then. Young girls
who loved words.
Girls who learned too early, like Marie,
how hard things are.

Fate's the handsome man at the party
no one knows anything about. He goes home
with the most unlikely girl.
Try to coax his secrets from him

and he'll embarrass you. As for second-guessing,
the odds are bad for everyone,

don't you think. Not even the lucky ones
know they're lucky.

It was years before I went to University,
got a boyfriend. Most of us so busy
trying to make the world fall in love with us
we couldn't tell one person

from another. "My mother left my father
for another man," Marie had told me.
I'd pictured everyone in that house
crowded in a cave drained of air.

But to take what's offered
with both hands, wasn't that the goal?
Everyone alive
was one of the chosen, I knew even then.

So when my boyfriend invited me over
I was too happy to think things through.
Thus it is willed
where everything may be

simply if it is willed.
(We were studying Dante in 101.)
Dante said, *Don't be deceived*
because the gate is wide.

In the field to the house, the only light
was the light I brought with me.
We played records. *Listen*, I said to my young self,
to the noise beneath the music.

I remember that evening,
the music a mirror. We took off our clothes.
"You seem to be enjoying this,"
my boyfriend said, smiling.

It isn't always possible to see things
right away. Or decide
how much you want to see. Or with whom.
Of course it ended terribly:

unhappiness, betrayal.
I still hear that music
when I'm falling asleep.
You will be brought to shore another way,

Dante said. *Someone is coming to open the city…*
As for Marie, last I heard,
she'd divorced,
fallen in love with a woman.

"You're not a real man at all,"
her mother had screamed at her father

years before. I was too young
to sympathize.

I just listened
as if Marie were telling
some preposterous story
using thrilling words: *adultery*, *affair*.

Marie knew secrets could enclose us
like slabs of granite. But words –
words could choose the moment, break it open
like a stonecutter.

We must have known, when we did give in,
the world would knock us around a bit. Back then,
it was enough to savour words. Words alone
kept us going for years.

LITTLE SISTER

Your heart is a horse
lame on the mudflats.
Let us rest where the dark
is immaculate. And even the last straw
is swept away.

SYNDROME

Lorraine, on the kitchen staff, doesn't talk much.
I look at her
as if from far away. What has she to do with me?

But later I will sit in circle
and learn her story.
She's so large.

"And I keep getting bigger," she says,
"so no one touches me." But once
someone touched her.

Even if you're abandoned, if you're in the garden
you can smell sweetness, hear
rustling. When an unexpected snow
covers the dahlias and they stay in bloom, you know

you're going to be okay.
For Lorraine the garden was
– snap. Anything could set her mother off

when she was drinking.
She'd see Lorraine playing in the mud
and she'd jump up, grab a stick. Whap.

No. But yes, she had to
let her mother. Otherwise

her little brother
would be the one to get it.

As the stick strikes her leg
what Lorraine hears – snow on dahlias.

That tree is staring at me. The big one
with the red eyes. I see it
from the window, Lorraine thinks.

"All trees are kind," her mother tells her,
"don't you know that?"

No one put salve on the cuts. In bed,
Lorraine shivers under thin covers.
That's when her mother crawls in beside her, wants to

hold her. What a pretty girl
with such a narrow waist. She slides her hand
across a shoulder.

There is silence
in which strength gathers. But there is another
more ominous silence
reminding you: the snowdrift is soundless
as it pulls you under.

Don't touch me, the girl shouts
but only in her head. She has not yet learned
to push against such force.

When she wakes she is no longer a girl
but a bear
walking in snow.

Some women walk
in frozen places.
They could continue that way forever
until they happen to look down
and see blood on the snow.

KIMBERLY ROGERS

You won't be there to greet her,
a woman alone and so big.
You will lose sight of her,
eight months pregnant in a bare
apartment. You will not be able to find her,
under house arrest, refrigerator

empty. She had undeclared student loans,
a judge who passed sentence: *You lied
and stole from your community*.
She had a mother she'd just reconciled with,
a government that cut off benefits, drugs
from her doctor.

You will not be the one to find
her decomposing body in the sweltering
apartment. Go meet her.
She is still in her room
where she made preparations. See how the baby
lies still in her belly,

how the body stays put
in the place it's assigned.
Just do not ask her
to get up and start over.

BLACK

Two women wearing silk gowns lounge
on a dark sheet that covers
an enormous bed. Blankets have
fallen. The women do not
go to the party to which they've been
invited. Though they have not yet
touched, what passes between them
is molten. *Lady, shall I lie
in your lap?* By dawn
one woman will be wearing only
stockings and garter. Who
is hurting whom? The one who loves
least, loses.

TO BREAK AWAY

She lives with her mother. Every Thursday
visits prison. *Hail Mary
Mother of God*, she prays. For one convict.
The Philosopher
she calls him. "Oh Danny Boy,"
he'd sing. Something
magnetic and forbidden
in that voice. She listens
for hours, says novenas

in his name. The trickster
spirit they call him. *No.*
The wrong God
they say. *No.* In that life
to follow
is to follow completely. The only witness,
the believer. He says her name softly, *Lia,* as if
it were full of secrets. It is all
holy ground – the prison, his release,
going back to the town he grew up in.
*I have a rendezvous with a woman
I've loved all my life and will never marry,*
he whispers. He'll be okay,

she thinks. She still thinks, then,
people say what they mean.
She's never met a man
who steals from himself.

How long after his release
does she get the letter?
Would you come down, retrieve the ashes?
his sister writes.
He requested this. It's in his will.
She is drinking tea, reading. That's when

she breaks the cup.
Who would narrow life down like that? she thinks.
To die by your own hand.

"You've never been on a plane before,"
her mother says.
Then it's high time. She is thirty-four.
"He was a convict, don't forget," her mother says.
He's dead, for Christ sake. Where's your charity?

There are places a woman cannot know she's crossed
until she crosses them. Then
she looks back and, how explain?

She gets off the plane. Yes. She is excited, nervous and.
She looks at the people waiting.
That's when she sees him – *not dead* – but waiting in a crowd
like anyone waiting.

Why burn and shiver too? She crosses herself
as he starts walking towards her. Then
she can't move.
Like a dream she lets him
bundle her into a car. From hotel to hotel.
For four months. Using her credit card. Each small thing,
enormous. By the time the police catch up with him
something is drawing to a close
around her.

Back home she stops fighting
to get things right.
Her mother is visiting a neighbour
when she stabs herself twice in the belly.

Born prematurely, weak lungs, the baby lives.
That's when William first sees her
in the incubator, ill. William –
the man who has come a long way
to adopt a baby. He picks her up,
holds her high. *Are you an evil looper
like your dad?* he wonders, staring

into the baby's face.
The infant shudders. That's when William
hugs her to his chest.
Some babies get a second chance,
new parents, new

stories. As for Ophelia,
one wonders what the world
would have offered her daughter.

SEX (OR WHEN WE WERE YOUNG)

When you tell this story
you remember how young you were.
What the hell, you thought,
it was your last night on shore

which gave you the courage to go up to her
when you saw her alone –
when would you have the chance again? –
so you left your pals, those guys from the ship,
and went over to her table.

That evening, the harbour
was dark glass floating between you
like ice. It magnified
a brilliant transparency.

After only one vodka, she said,
"Yes, I'll have dinner with you." But in the taxi,
her blonde hair like a cloud,
her eyes pale, she turned to you suddenly and laughed –
"Do you really want to have dinner, or should we just
go to my place and..."

Light ignited the embers in her hay-coloured hair
like dry tinder.

There's desire to release, at whatever cost,
all that's kept hidden in what's frozen. Then the urge
retreats. Then the urge is lost.

You describe a woman who is not here.
What can you say, except,
How would she have told her story?

MEMO

Did I get it wrong? The moon's steely light
covering your face,
lighting and shading it. Not anger
but helplessness damping a light
inside you. The water's glossy surface, your
only unbroken home. Those silent
meals, the dressing, undressing. Restraint
smothering the day
like gravel. Gravel you spit out: words
unsaid. All this exists
only in my mind. As you were born
in someone else's. The images I steal –
you in blue light kneeling in snow, praying
to escape where you didn't want to go –
these reveal in high relief, not you (so you tell me)
but my own impenetrable longings.
That's what makes you real, Ophelia.

FOR A DROWNED WOMAN

I've learned
where I can lead a horse.
What I did not know
is how you, yourself, would drink me up
as verse, as psalm. Or that,
when the river sobbed, I would get it in my head
to swim in you. In you
the wrestling, a restless
knotting, an endless blue. And if you are only
words, what else, well chosen, sustains
better on this steep incline?
We've taken hold of each other
as if weather or hunger or fever
could not rob us. As if we will not vanish
like water that quenches thirst
or drains into the earth in its riverbed.

WHAT I COULD HAVE LEARNED BY THE LIGHT OF MISFORTUNE

came to me instead in a copse of trees
when the self and the half-eaten starling in the dirt,
the clamour of a drunk man arguing with himself, the call
of a bird *hi sweetie* and the certainty

that I would not be here much longer
were the same, the door of the self
temporarily torn off its hinges.
What entered then

did not leave; *does anything leave?*
I knew then that when I listened to trees
as if overhearing a private conversation, their chatter
was not as intimate as their silence,

not as intimate as the luck and shock I felt
each time I was caught that summer
by the elegance of blood-red Japanese maples
standing among oak and aspen and pine.

NOTHING HELD YOU

By your loss, you instructed me.

From the weeping sky
to the old sea that broods, steeped
and repeating invocations. From the astounding blue
at day's end, to each new day's
slew of losses, ground down
in gold and rust, longing
sheer and harsh as storm. It's fierce,
Ophelia, what keeps us here: Everything
that holds, reaches, not around
but through us.

NOTES & ACKNOWLEDGEMENTS

SPY
"The spy designs himself to be overlooked" is a quotation from Jasper Johns and can be found in *Jasper Johns: Writings, Sketchbook Notes, Interviews* (The Museum of Modern Art, 2002).

COCK
The italicized line is a play on "For some must watch, while some must sleep" from Shakespeare's *Hamlet*, Act 3, Scene 2.

YAHRZEIT
Yahrzeit: the Jewish custom of observing the death of a close relative.

Minyan: the number of persons required by Jewish Law to be present for a religious service, at least ten males over thirteen years of age.

Mikvah: a ritual bath in naturally collected water, considered a necessary preparation (for spiritual as well as physical cleansing) before getting married.

THE MOVIE
With thanks to Mark Palermo for his movie reviews.

OPHELIA'S INTERVIEW WITH CARL JUNG
Thanks to the brilliant Anne Carson for "Interview with Hara Tamiki (1950)."

WHEN HE CROSSED THE FIELD
The italicized line is a quotation from Vincent van Gogh in a letter to his brother Theo.

HEART'S OVEN
For the idea in the last stanza, thanks to Larry McMurtry and *Lonesome Dove*.

SHOULD TWO ARMS LIFT ME
This poem was written in response to Millais' *Ophelia*, painted in 1852.

KIMBERLY ROGERS
Kimberly Rogers committed suicide in 2001 in her Sudbury apartment, destitute and eight months pregnant, while under house arrest for welfare fraud.

BLACK
This poem was inspired by a movie review by David Denby. The italicized line in the poem is a quote from *Hamlet*, Act 3, Scene 2.

TO BREAK AWAY
"*I have a rendezvous with a woman I've loved all my life and will never marry*" is a quotation from John Berger, taken from *Selected Essays* (Vintage International, 2001).

"Pastor" Robert Delford Brown, a performance artist whose motto was "Everything is art, everyone is an artist; there is no not art," founded "The First Church of the Exquisite Panic, Inc" on West 13th Street in 1964. Thanks to my sister Barbara Glasser for telling me about this church.

Some of these poems (or versions of them) have been published in the following journals and anthologies: *The Antigonish Review, Canadian Woman Studies, Cahoots, In Fine Form: The Canadian Book of Form Poetry* (Polestar, 2005), *The Malahat Review, Our Times, Stony Thursday Book, Sudden Thunder Anthology* (Silver Bow Publishing, 2011), *Ellipse, Stone Voices*.

Ten poems from this book were shortlisted for the CBC Literary Award for Poetry.

"Not" was put to music by the composer Alice Ho and performed by Janice Jackson.

To these gifted and generous poets: Thank you Stan Dragland for unlocking secrets about this manuscript and having faith in it. Thank you Alexandra Thurman and Karin Cope for helping me find an order, Jan Zwicky for your early support of *Church of the Exquisite Panic* and your comments, Matilka Krow for inspiring me, Lorri Neilson Glen, Kathy Mac and Matilka, for reading these poems years ago and making suggestions. Alayna Munce, thank you for your brilliant editing and suggestions. Beth Follett for getting, right away, what I was trying to do here. Thank you.

PHOTO Karen Runge

Church of the Exquisite Panic: The Ophelia Poems is Carole Glasser Langille's fourth book of poetry. She has been nominated for the Governor General's Award and the Atlantic Poetry Prize. Six poems from her last book of poems, *Late in a Slow Time,* were put to music by the composer Chan Ka Nin and recorded by Duo Concertante. Her most recent book is a collection of short stories, *When I Always Wanted Something.* She has taught at Humber School for Writers Summer Workshop, and given readings in India, the Czech Republic and Greece. She teaches Creative Writing at Dalhousie University.